Mother-Daughter Book Club Guide

Building Connection & Community

Meghan Voss
Stefanie Hohl

Playful Learning Press

Mother-Daughter Book Club Guide
Copyright © 2025 by Meghan Voss and Stefanie Hohl

All rights reserved. Printed in the United States of America.

No part of this book may be used or reproduced in any manner without written permission.

For information regarding permission, go to www.stefaniehohl.com.

Summary: A guide for planning Mother-Daughter Book Club events including book summaries, discussion questions, snacks, and ideas for activities.

ISBN: 978-1-63824-054-9

Dedication

MV: To Pepper—keep asking all the questions!

SH: To Kaitlin and all our Book Club Friends

Table of Contents

PART 1: Helpful Information
- Building Connection & Community
- Who Can Use This Book
- What's Included
- Tips for Launching YOUR Book Club
- Tips for Hosts
- Activity Ideas for Any Book
- A Note from the Authors

PART 2: The Guide
- *The True Confessions of Charlotte Doyle* by Avi 13
- *Inside Out and Back Again* by Thanhhà Lại 19
- *Out of My Mind* by Sharon M. Draper 25
- *Three Times Lucky* by Sheila Turnage 31
- *Smile* by Raina Telgemeier 37
- *Princess Academy* by Shannon Hale 43
- *Where the Mountain Meets the Moon* by Grace Lin 49
- *Keeper of the Lost Cities* by Shannon Messenger 55
- *Anne of Green Gables* by L. M. Montgomery 61
- *Bridge to Terabithia* by Katherine Paterson 67
- *I Am Malala: How One Girl Stood Up for Education and Changed the World* by Malala Yousafzai 73
- *Yummy: A History of Desserts* by Victoria Elliott 79

APPENDIX
- Index
- About the Authors

PART I

Helpful Information

Part 1: Helpful Information

Book Clubs:
Building Connection & Community

It's no secret that reading books with children is a great way to connect, build memories, and instill a lifelong love of literature. Involving kids in book clubs fosters even greater literacy confidence by incorporating critical thinking skills and multiple learning modalities, all while strengthening family relationships and promoting community-building.

But in a society full of screens, activities, and other distractions, prioritizing reading and celebrating books can prove challenging. Even the most dedicated parents end up feeling overwhelmed by the hundreds of titles to choose from, not to mention the daunting task of sorting through activity ideas on the internet.

That's where we come in!

Our parent/child book club guides allow hosts to easily plan fun and interactive book club meetings—because we do all the work for you! For each of our curated book suggestions, we've compiled discussion questions, easy snack ideas, simple activities, and more.

Does your daughter love to plan? Give her this book and let her go for it! This not only empowers your daughter in her love of literacy–it also builds leadership skills and responsibility!

With our guides, kids will:
- Get off screens and into books
- Build friendships
- Learn empathy by reading a wide variety of stories
- Develop critical reading and thinking skills

Mother-Daughter book clubs benefit parents, too! Our guides will help parents:

- Prioritize reading time with reading goals and timelines
- Create a community around books and idea-sharing
- Build meaningful friendships
- Strengthen parent-child relationships
- Inspire a lifelong love of books, critical thinking, and connection

With many more guides planned for this series, you'll have countless ideas and suggestions to try. The sky's the limit!

Who Can Use this Book

The *Mother/Daughter Book Club Guide* isn't just for mothers and daughters! Fathers, sons, homeschool parents, and all kinds of educators can benefit from the ideas we've included in this guide. We love it when librarians, storytime leaders, teachers, and book event planners have fun with our suggestions!

What's Included

Book Choices: These books are designed to appeal to 9-12 year olds. We recognize that this is a large age range, so we encourage facilitators to use careful judgment when deciding whether their daughter/group is ready for each book. While we offer book-specific age guides, each child is different and will respond as such.

Discussion Questions: Each book includes a list of questions to spark thought and discussion. Depending on the goals of your group, you may decide to focus on more intellectual or more "fun" questions. In any case, we hope the questions allow participants to practice critical thinking skills as they apply literary concepts to their life.

Activities: Activities are a great way to make literature fun and memorable! We've included a list of simple, book-related activities for each book. Feel free to use just one option, a few options, or to use our suggestions as a jumping-off point for your own ideas.

Snacks: What's a book club without snacks? For each book, we've included snack ideas that go along with the story. We couldn't include every food item mentioned in every book—those lists would be way too long!—but we've got plenty of creative ideas to get you started. Some snack suggestions relate to recipes that are included in the books themselves, while others may require an internet search.

Fun Facts: Each book includes interesting facts about the book and/or the author.

Picture Book Suggestions: Each book includes picture book suggestions. Use these to spark discussion by comparing and contrasting themes and topics found in the longer book. For example, after reading the book *Inside Out and Back Again*, reading a picture book about a refugee or cultural divides can help broaden and deepen group discussion.

Tips for Launching YOUR Book Club

1. **Define Your Goals:** Every book club is different, and that's okay! Is your endgame to foster a love of reading, strengthen friendships and mother-daughter relationships, or to encourage good discussions? Being specific with your goals will help you focus on what success looks like for your group.
2. **Find Participants:** Reach out to other moms with daughters of a similar age—perhaps through a school class, church group, or other activity group. A group of 5-8 mother/daughter pairs is ideal, but feel free to include as few or as many people as you'd like!
3. **Choose Meeting Frequency:** Do you want to meet monthly, every six weeks, or every other month? Maybe every week in the summer? There's no wrong answer. Choose what works best for you!
4. **Create a Schedule:** Who will host each month? What day and time will you meet? Taking the time to plan about 3-6 months in advance makes a *huge* difference.
5. **Select Books:** There are many ways to do this, but these are our favorite methods:
   ◇ Vote on books for the whole year at once.
   ◇ Vote at the end of each meeting for the next month.
   ◇ Let the host family choose the next book.
6. **Communication:** Once your group is ready to get started, decide how to communicate important information. Some ideas include evites, text messages, email, or social media groups. It's most helpful if one person is in charge of sending out info and reminders.
7. **Structure:** It's always a good idea to decide on a loose structure for each book club meeting. How much time do you hope to spend on discussion, snacks, and/or

activities? This way, hosts and guests know what to expect and can plan accordingly.
8. **Choose a Name for Your Book Club:** Get creative and have fun with this! Great names inspire fun and community!
9. **Be Flexible:** Life happens! Some meetings will be flawless, and some will be chaotic. Group members will come and go. People may not like the books you choose, you might forget the snack altogether, and there could even be some awkward social drama. Remind yourself that it's all part of the process, and imperfection is not only okay, but it often results in the best memories!

Tips for Hosts

1. Read through the book summaries and stats as you choose which books to read and when to read them. A grief book right before the holidays might not be the best experience, but a family-centered book could be perfect!
2. Prepare for book club meetings by reading through all the material for your chosen book in advance. Activity and snack planning may require an extra internet search and/or trip to the store, so give yourself time to prepare.
3. Let your creative juices flow! This is a guidebook, not a rulebook. Always feel free to adapt our ideas to meet the needs of your group, and never resist allowing the ideas in this guidebook to inspire your own ideas. We'd love to hear about them—please share and tag us!

Activity Ideas for Any Book

- Make a movie trailer for the book
- Contact the author for a virtual book club visit
- Watch the movie (if there is one)
- Take a book club field trip: get creative with this idea, depending on which book you're reading and where you live
- Attend an author event
- Play book-themed Charades
- Make bookmarks based on the book
- Make character puppets
- Act out favorite scenes from the book
- Draw or paint favorite scenes or characters in the book
- Create a book collage with magazine clippings
- Plan a scavenger hunt for items related to the book
- Play book-themed Bingo
- "Cast" the characters with actual actors/celebrities

A Note from the Authors

When it comes to books, Stef and Meg have been connected for as long as they can remember.

As a child, Meg wrote all kinds of stories that her younger sister Stef eagerly gobbled up before begging for more. Stef's enthusiastic response helped propel Meg into a life of books, writing, and teaching. With a Masters degree in education and a career spanning secondary teaching, tutoring, freelance writing, and professional editing, Meg is passionate about helping kids and teens love literature and writing—and helping them believe they can create it, too!

By the time Stef became a mom, her bookish enthusiasm meant her house was stacked to the brim with books and reading. So when her eight-year-old daughter declared she hated reading, Stef was horrified! To entice her social butterfly back into the world of books, Stef launched her first Mother-Daughter book club with themed snacks and activities.

That decision was a game-changer—more than a decade later, her daughter still reads voraciously and calls Stef to discuss books!

Stef has hosted everything from Mother-Daughter and Mother-Son book clubs to church and friend book clubs, in addition to earning multiple Masters degrees in literacy-related subjects. She and Meg have cheered each other on as they've continued to work together as writing partners, business partners, friends, and sisters.

Now that Meg's oldest daughter is reading chapter books, it seemed perfectly appropriate to partner once again—this time to publish their first Mother-Daughter Book Club Guide together!

We hope you will love this guide. In creating this project, our overarching goal has always been to help moms and daughters cultivate connection, community, and lasting memories of bookish joy.

PART II

The Guide

The True Confessions of Charlotte Doyle
by Avi

In this swashbuckling murder mystery, thirteen-year-old Charlotte Doyle unexpectedly finds herself the sole passenger on a ship bound from England to her home in Rhode Island. When she finds proof of a planned mutiny, she dutifully notifies Captain Jaggery—who reacts with a cruelty Charlotte never expected. Caught between Captain Jaggery and his vengeful crew, Charlotte must decide whether doing the right thing is worth risking not only her reputation, but her life.

Avi. *The True Confessions of Charlotte Doyle*. New York: Scholastic, 1990.

STATS
- Genre: Historical Fiction, 1832
- Subgenre: Mystery, Nautical Fiction
- Themes: Courage, Class, Gender
- Page Count: 226
- Best for Ages: 10+

AWARDS & LISTS
- 1991 Newbery Honor
- Golden Kite Award
- Boston Globe-Horn Book Award
- ALA Notable Children's Book

DISCUSSION QUESTIONS

1. Have you ever been blamed for something you didn't do? How did that make you feel?
2. How does Charlotte change from the beginning to the end of the book?
3. Charlotte was trapped between two worlds—which world would you prefer to belong to and why?
4. Imagine Charlotte's future life. Where do you think she will end up?
5. Why do you think Zachariah chose to trust Charlotte, even though no one else did?
6. At the end of the book, Charlotte remembers something Zachariah told her: " 'A sailor,' he said, 'chooses the wind that takes the ship from safe port… but winds have a mind of their own' " (210). What do you think Zachariah meant by that? How do you see this happening in Charlotte's life? Have you ever been surprised by where your choices have led?
7. Knowing what you know now, what advice would you give Charlotte before she gets on Captain Jaggery's ship?
8. How would Charlotte's life have changed if her parents had listened to her at the end? Do you wish they had? Why or why not?
9. Charlotte exercised both moral courage (standing up for what's right) AND physical courage (scaling the ship's rigging). What are some ways you can show moral courage in your life? What about physical courage?
10. When Charlotte's father burned her journals, she used pages of books to rewrite everything she could remember, because "it was my way of fixing all the details in my mind forever" (208). Why was writing her story so important to Charlotte? Why might it be helpful to write down your life experiences?

SNACK IDEAS
- **Hardtack or Sailor's Bread:** Add a dab of molasses for more flavor!
- **Sugar cookies:** Decorate them with the round robin from the book (image on p. 46 of the 2012 edition)
- **Tea**
- **Boiled meat, rice, and beans**
- **Sailor's Duff or Seaman's Delight:** Recipe is included in the Afterword of the 2012 edition of the book

ACTIVITY IDEAS
- **Journal Decorating:** Purchase a notebook for each girl and decorate the covers using scrapbook paper, stickers, markers, etc.
- **Knot Tying:** Learn to tie sailors' knots! Directions for a few knots are included in the Afterword of the 2012 edition.
- **Ship Drawing:** Draw and label the parts of a 19th-century sailing ship. Directions are included in the Afterword of the 2012 edition.
- **Mock Trial:** Hold a mock trial for the murder of Mr. Hollybrass! Each girl can play a different character—Charlotte, Captain Jaggery, Mr. Dillingham, Mr. Ewing, Mr. Grimes, Mr. Barlow, etc.—with mothers acting as judge and jury.
- **Climb the Rigging:** If a playground or climbing wall is available, let each girl pretend to climb the rigging of the ship to touch the topmost spar of the royal yard.

IF YOU LIKED THIS BOOK, YOU'LL LOVE...
- *Three Times Lucky* by Sheila Turnage
- *Princess Academy* by Shannon Hale

FUN FACTS
- Born Edward Irving Wortis, the author's twin sister gave him the nickname "Avi" as a child.
- This book was inspired by Edgar Allan Poe's invention of the "locked-room mystery." In a locked-room mystery, a crime takes place in a sealed location, so it's "impossible" for the perpetrator to get in, commit the crime, and escape. Avi thought a ship would be a perfect setting for such a story.
- Avi has published 80 books! He won a Newbery Honor for *Nothing but the Truth* in 1992, and a Newbery Medal for *Crispin: The End of Time* in 2003.

PICTURE BOOK SUGGESTIONS
- *Swashby and the Sea* by Beth Ferry
- *Sail* by Dorien Brouwers

The True Confessions of Charlotte Doyle
Planning Guide

Meeting Date & Time: _____

Host: _____

Rating: ☆☆☆☆☆

Thoughts about the Book:

_____

_____

_____

Snacks:

_____

_____

_____

Activities:

_____

_____

_____

Supplies Needed:

_____

_____

_____

Notes:

_____

_____

_____

How Did It Go?

_____

_____

_____

Future Planning

Next Book: _____

Next Meeting Time: _____

Next Host: _____

Part 2: The Guide

Inside Out and Back Again
by Thanhhà Lại

War rages in Vietnam, and Hà's mother anxiously awaits news from her husband, who has been missing in action for years. But when Saigon falls to the Communists, Hà's mother makes the difficult choice to flee their beloved homeland. Hà, her mother, and her three brothers must endure a refugee camp and a cramped ocean crossing—but due to bullies, a new language, and the loneliness of a brand-new culture, their new life in America might prove the biggest challenge of all.

Lại, Thanhhà. *Inside Out & Back Again*. New York: HarperCollins, 2011.

STATS
- Publisher: HarperCollins
- Originally Published: 2011
- Genre: Historical Fiction, 1975
- Subgenre: Novel in Verse
- Themes: Immigrant Story, Bullying, Culture, Friendship
- Page Count: 260
- Best for Ages: 9+

AWARDS & LISTS
- National Book Award for Young People's Literature
- 2012 Newbery Honor

DISCUSSION QUESTIONS

1. Whom would you like as your friend? Scrappy Hà, intellectual Quang, soft-hearted Khôi, or cool Vu Lee? Why?
2. Why did Hà give her doll to Khôi after his chick died? Why do you think her kindness helped him heal?
3. "So this is/ what dumb/ feels like./ I hate, hate, hate it" (157). Why does Hà feel dumb? Have you ever felt dumb before? Why? What can we learn from Hà's situation?
4. What can Hà's experience teach us about how to treat people who are different than we are?
5. How would you feel if you had to learn a new language at a new school? What could other people do to make your experience easier?
6. Hà calls the day she eats Mrs. Washington's lunch in her classroom and meets Pam and Steven "Most Relieved Day" (p.185). Why?
7. When did Mother finally know that Father had died? How did that realization change her and her family?
8. In what ways did Hà show strength and courage in spite of the hard things she was experiencing? How can you show courage when life is hard?
9. At the end of the story, Hà prays for something meaningful for each of her family members, and then she prays for something meaningful for herself. She says, "This year I hope/ I truly learn/ to fly-kick,/ not to kick anyone/so much as/ to fly" (259-260). What do you think she means by that? What kind of "gift" would you choose for your family members at the start of a new year? What "New Year's gift" would you hope for yourself?
10. What do you think Hà's next year of school in America will bring? What will change? What will stay the same?

SNACK IDEAS
- **Rice**
- **Papaya**
- **Sugary fried dough**
- **Mung bean cookies**
- **Sweet bubbly drinks**
- **Ramen noodles**

ACTIVITY IDEAS
- **Write a Poem:** Challenge the girls to write a poem about a pivotal moment in their life. Encourage them to share their poems if they want to.
- **Learn Self-Defense:** Watch a video on self-defense. Then practice the moves together!
- **Family Stories:** Ask the girls to bring a family story to share. They can create a slideshow, show photos, or bring other items to share about their family history.
- **Learn Vietnamese:** Hà struggles to learn English. Learn Vietnamese words together and imagine how hard it would be to move to a new country where you didn't speak the language.
- **Plant a Tree or Flowers:** Hà loved her papaya tree and planted flowers in memory of her father. Let each girl plant flowers in a small planter to take home.

FUN FACTS
- Thanhhà Lại chose to write this novel in verse because the poetic prose in English is similar to the way she thinks in lyrical Vietnamese.
- Thanhhà Lại was also a Vietnamese refugee! While the story is fiction, Thanhhà Lại based many of Hà's experiences on her own childhood.
- Thanhhà Lại founded an organization called Viet Kids to provide kids in Vietnam with bicycles, rice, and scholarships. She donates all of her school visit fees to Viet Kids.

IF YOU LIKED THIS BOOK, YOU'LL LOVE...
- *I am Malala: How One Girl Stood Up for Education and Changed the World (Young Reader's Edition)* by Malala Yousefzai
- *Princess Academy* by Shannon Hale

PICTURE BOOK SUGGESTIONS
- *Drawn Together* by Minh Lê
- *What is a Refugee?* By Elise Gravel

Inside Out and Back Again
Planning Guide

Meeting Date & Time: _____

Host: _____

Rating: ☆☆☆☆☆

Thoughts about the Book:

_____

_____

_____

Snacks:

_____

_____

_____

Activities:

_____

_____

_____

Supplies Needed:

_____

_____

_____

Notes:

_____

_____

_____

How Did It Go?

_____

_____

_____

Future Planning

Next Book: _____

Next Meeting Time: _____

Next Host: _____

Out of My Mind
by Sharon M. Draper

As much as she wants to fit in, Melody is used to being different. Though her brain is full of words, colors, music, and knowledge, she's never been able to share any of it. Born with cerebral palsy, Melody's physical impairments make it impossible for her to speak. So when she learns about a device that will allow her to express her ideas, she can't wait to try it. With the help of her Medi-talker, Melody defies school bullies and disbelieving teachers to join the school Whiz Kids Quiz Team. Will this feat finally convince people to include her?

Draper, Sharon M. *Out of My Mind*. New York: Atheneum Books for Young Readers, 2010.

STATS
- Publisher: Atheneum Books for Young Readers
- Originally Published: 2010
- Genre: Realistic Fiction
- Subgenre: Disabilities
- Themes: Diversity, Kindness, Inclusion
- Page Count: 295
- Best for Ages: 9+

AWARDS & LISTS
- New York Times Bestseller
- Kirkus Reviews Best Book of 2010

DISCUSSION QUESTIONS

1. How would you feel if you couldn't talk? What would be the first thing you would say?
2. Melody says she "can almost hear colors and smell images when music is played" (5). Mom's classical music is bright blue and smells like "fresh paint," Dad's jazz music is brown and tan and smells like "wet dirt," and country music is "cool, fresh lemonade!" (6). What is your favorite type of music? How would you describe its color, taste, or smell?
3. Melody feels badly for her goldfish because it's stuck in a bowl with no way to escape. How is this similar to Melody's experience?
4. Sometimes Melody feels jealous of her sister because she can do things easily that Melody can't do. Have you ever felt jealous of a friend or sibling? How did you work through it?
5. In what ways did Melody's teacher and classmates underestimate her? Have you ever underestimated someone else?
6. "I suppose it's a good thing to be. . . able to keep every instant of my life crammed inside my head. But it's also very frustrating" (7). Do you wish you could remember everything that happened in your life? Why or why not?
7. How can we help other people feel included—at home, at school, or with friends?
8. How does Melody change from the beginning to the end of the book?
9. How did Mrs. V's challenges help Melody get stronger?
10. Mrs. V tells Claire, "Some people get braces on their teeth. Some get braces on their legs. For others, braces won't work, so they need wheelchairs and walkers and such. You're a lucky girl that you only had messed-up teeth. Remember that" (120). What are some things that you take for granted in your life?

SNACK IDEAS
- **Applesauce**
- **Oatmeal or Cream of Wheat**
- **Big Mac and vanilla shake**
- **Chocolate chip cookies and milk**
- **Macaroni and cheese**
- **Pizza**

ACTIVITY IDEAS
- **Quiz Game:** Create a quiz game, using questions about the book or random trivia.
- **Communication Game:** Divide girls into groups of two or three. Give each group a sheet of paper filled with words. Instruct each girl to take a turn communicating a sentence using only their thumbs to point to words.
- **Feed Each Other:** Take turns feeding each other snacks. The girl being fed must keep her hands behind her back. Discuss how challenging this was.
- **Music Listening:** Listen to different types of music—what colors or smells does each style of music make you think about?
- **Invent Technology:** Melody's life is greatly improved by Elvira. Come up with an invention that could help with one or more disabilities. Draw your invention or build it out of recycled materials. Get creative!

FUN FACTS
- *Out of My Heart* is the sequel to *Out of My Mind*.
- Like Melody, Sharon M. Draper's daughter has cerebral palsy. Sharon was inspired to write this book to help others better understand people with disabilities.
- Not only is Sharon M. Draper a five-time winner of the Coretta Scott King Literary Award, but she also taught high school English for over twenty-five years and was named National Teacher of the Year in 1997!

IF YOU LIKED THIS BOOK, YOU'LL LOVE…
- *Smile* by Raina Telgemeier
- *Anne of Green Gables* by L. M. Montgomery

PICTURE BOOK SUGGESTIONS
- *When Charley Met Emma* by Amy Webb
- *Brilliant Bea* by Shaina Rudolph

Part 2: The Guide

Out of My Mind
Planning Guide

Meeting Date & Time: _____

Host: _____

Rating: ☆☆☆☆☆

Thoughts about the Book:

_____

_____

_____

Snacks:

_____

_____

_____

Activities:

_____

_____

_____

Supplies Needed:

_____

_____

_____

Notes:

_____

_____

_____

How Did It Go?

_____

_____

_____

Future Planning

Next Book:_____

Next Meeting Time:_____

Next Host:_____

Three Times Lucky
by Sheila Turnage

When Moses "Mo" LeBeau was just a baby, she washed up onto the banks of Tupelo Landing during a hurricane. Desperate to learn about her mysterious roots, Mo sends messages in bottles with the hope of one day finding her Upstream Mother. But when a big city detective comes into town to investigate a murder, Mo and her best friend Dale decide to expand their sleuthing. The newly-minted Desperado Detectives get themselves in and out of scrapes as they attempt to get to the bottom of Tupelo Landing's biggest scandal.

Turnage, Sheila. *Three Times Lucky*. New York: Dial Books for Young Readers, 2012.

STATS
- Publisher: The Penguin Group
- Originally Published: 2012
- Genre: Realistic Fiction
- Subgenre: Mystery
- Themes: Found Family, Friendship, Community
- Page Count: 312
- Best for Ages: 9+

AWARDS & LISTS
- 2013 Newbery Honor Book
- New York Times Bestseller
- Edgar Award Finalist
- E.B. White Read Aloud Honor Book

DISCUSSION QUESTIONS

1. Did you trust Detective Joe Starr at the beginning of the novel? Why or why not?
2. Miss Lana and the Colonel claim that Mo is *three times lucky*. Do you agree that Mo was lucky? Why or why not?
3. How does the hurricane add extra excitement to the end of the story? Why are storms important to Mo and the Colonel?
4. " 'You try to figure out your life every time you get close to a birthday, Mo, and you ain't done it yet. I wish you'd leave it alone,' [Dale] said, slumping against the door. 'I'm tired of hearing about it. There's nothing wrong with the people you got' " (52). Why is Dale sick of Mo looking for her Upstream Mother? Why does Mo feel differently? Do you think Mo should end her search?
5. This book has lots of interesting characters, from Miss Lana to the Colonel, Valentine, Miss Rose, and even Anna Celeste! Who were your favorites? Why?
6. What theme would *you* choose for the cafe? How would you and Miss Lana pull it off? Which decorations/costumes would you use?
7. Were you surprised to find out Deputy Marla was in on the heist? If not, what tipped you off?
8. Would you enjoy living in Tupelo Landing? Why or why not?
9. When Mo feels scared about Miss Lana being lost, she looks at the night sky and remembers the Colonel's words: " 'When you feel lost, let the stars sing you to sleep. You'll always wake up new. Do you understand what I'm telling you, Soldier?' 'I think I do now, Sir,' I whispered" (214). What do you think those words mean to Mo? What do they mean to you?
10. Do you think Mo will ever find her Upstream Mother? If she does, how will her life change?

SNACK IDEAS
- **Peanut butter banana sandwich**, hand-squished or fluffy
- **Garden soup**, served cold
- **Apple pie with ice cream**
- **Picnic fixin's!** Fried chicken, deviled eggs, coleslaw, potato salad, rolls
- **Oreos, cheese puffs, chips, pretzels**

ACTIVITY IDEAS
- **Message in a Bottle:** Buy glass bottles at the dollar store. Have the girls write messages to their future selves. Decorate the bottles, seal the messages inside, and instruct the girls to open the bottles when they graduate from high school.
- **Piggly Wiggly Chronicles:** Give each girl a notebook to decorate. Tell them to use it to write their autobiography or letters to family members they've never met.
- **Karate Night:** Watch videos online—then practice basic karate and self-defense moves!
- **Café:** Set up a pretend café with a Paris theme. Let the girls order and serve food to each other.
- **Detective Agency:** Split the girls into groups to create their own detective agencies! Challenge them to come up with a name, a slogan, and a business card design.

FUN FACTS
- This is the first book in the Mo and Dale Mystery series. The next three books are *The Ghosts of Tupelo Landing*, *The Odds of Getting Even*, and *The Law of Finders Keepers*.
- Before she knew the rest of the story, Mo's voice came to Sheila Turnage. When she started writing in that voice, the rest is history!
- Sheila Turnage grew up on a farm in North Carolina.

IF YOU LIKED THIS BOOK, YOU'LL LOVE...
- *Princess Academy* by Shannon Hale
- *Anne of Green Gables* by L. M. Montgomery

PICTURE BOOK SUGGESTIONS
- *A Family Like Ours* by Frank Murphy and Alice Lee
- *A Family is a Family is a Family* by Sara O'Leary

Part 2: The Guide

Three Times Lucky
Planning Guide

Meeting Date & Time: _____

Host: _____

Rating: ☆☆☆☆☆

Thoughts about the Book:

_____

_____

_____

Snacks:

_____

_____

_____

Activities:

_____

_____

_____

Supplies Needed:

_____

_____

_____

Notes:

_____

_____

_____

How Did It Go?

_____

_____

_____

Future Planning

Next Book: _____
Next Meeting Time: _____
Next Host: _____

Smile
by Raina Telgemeier

Sixth grader Raina can't wait to be a teenager—until she knocks out her front teeth in a painful fall! Faced with years of corrective dental work, Raina is devastated to realize that her teen years won't look the way she's always imagined them. But as years pass and friendships shift and grow, Raina realizes that getting her smile back means more than her physical appearance.

Telgemeier, Raina. *Smile*. New York: Scholastic, 2010.

STATS
- Publisher: Scholastic
- Originally Published: 2010
- Genre: Memoir
- Subgenre: Graphic Novel
- Themes: Coming of Age, Friendship, Kindness
- Page Count: 224
- Best for Ages: 9+

AWARDS & LISTS
- New York Times Bestseller
- 2010 Boston Globe–Horn Book Honor for Nonfiction
- Young Adult Library Service Association 2011 Top Ten Graphic Novels for Teens
- Eisner Award

DISCUSSION QUESTIONS

1. Raina says getting her ears pierced makes her feel like a real teenager. What do you think would make you feel like a real teenager?
2. In what ways did breaking her front teeth change Raina's life? In what ways did her life stay the same?
3. Raina didn't always want to admit it, but she loved *The Little Mermaid* movie. Did you ever have a favorite show or movie that might be embarrassing to admit?
4. Raina's "friends" tell her she needs to be less sensitive and laugh when they do mean things. How would you feel if you were in Raina's shoes? What would you do?
5. How did Raina's high school friends differ from her middle school friends? What characteristics make someone a good friend?
6. Was Raina's smile worth all that pain and effort? Why or why not?
7. Raina really likes some parts of being a teenager and really dislikes other parts of teenage life. Which parts of childhood do you love? What don't you like?
8. When Raina ditches her old friends, she thinks, "It was a little lonely now and then, but it didn't bother me./ I was happy to take life at my very own pace" (193). By giving up her friends, what else did Raina have to give up? What did she gain?
9. As Raina grows up, she realizes that art is one of her favorite things to do. What are some of your favorite hobbies?
10. When Raina smiled at the end of the book, she realized that she was finally smiling on the outside *and* the inside. Think of a time when you felt happy on the outside and the inside. What happened?

SNACK IDEAS
- **Ice cream**
- **Chicken broth**
- **Soft foods:** Oatmeal, yogurt, applesauce, macaroni and cheese, soup, scrambled eggs, mashed potatoes

ACTIVITY IDEAS
- **Make Fake Teeth:** Use Chiclets or Starbursts to mold fake front teeth on top of your own. Get creative with your smiles and take photos!
- **Passions:** Raina became more confident and happy when she started focusing on things she liked, rather than her outward appearance. Write a list of things you are passionate about or things you're interested in learning. Make a goal to work on one of these things.
- **Write a Memoir:** Write and draw a short story about something that happened to you, graphic novel style! If you'd like, read your stories to each other.
- **Compliment Papers:** Write each girl's name on the top of a piece of paper. Pass the papers around and invite everyone to write what they like about the person listed on the paper. Each girl can take home a paper full of nice things about themselves.
- **Kindness Bracelets:** Make bracelets out of embroidery thread and letter beads. Each girl chooses a kind word to spell out on a bracelet (words like "strong," "smart," "funny," "nice," etc.). Encourage them to give their bracelet to a friend.

FUN FACTS
- Based on her own teen experience, this graphic-novel memoir was both written and illustrated by the author.
- It takes Raina 2-5 years to write and illustrate a graphic novel!

IF YOU LIKED THIS BOOK, YOU'LL LOVE...
- *Yummy, a History of Desserts* by Victoria Grace Elliott
- *Out of My Mind* by Sharon M. Draper

PICTURE BOOK SUGGESTIONS
- *Alan's Big Scary Teeth* by Jarvis
- *I Am Enough* by Grace Byers

Smile
Planning Guide

Meeting Date & Time: _____

Host: _____

Rating: ☆☆☆☆☆

Thoughts about the Book:

_____

_____

_____

Snacks:

_____

_____

_____

Activities:

_____

_____

Supplies Needed:

_____

_____

_____

Notes:

_____

_____

_____

How Did It Go?

_____

_____

_____

Future Planning

Next Book: _____
Next Meeting Time: _____
Next Host: _____

Princess Academy
by Shannon Hale

When the chief delegate of Danland announces that the new princess will be selected from Miri's tiny mining town, Miri is *not* impressed. All she wants is her father's permission to work in the quarry, just like everyone else. Instead, Miri and all the other Mt. Eskel girls must attend Princess Academy to prepare for the prince's ball. As days turn into weeks and months away from home, Miri considers life outside of her mountain while unexpectedly learning secrets about the silent language of the Mt. Eskel quarry. In time, all her learning will be put to the test—both for the chance to become a princess and to save the girls of Mt. Eskel.

Hale, Shannon. *Princess Academy*. New York: Bloomsbury, 2005.

STATS
- Publisher: Bloomsbury
- Originally Published: 2005
- Genre: Fantasy
- Subgenre: Adventure
- Themes: Courage, Believing in Yourself, Friendship, Education
- Page Count: 314
- Best for Ages: 9+

AWARDS & LISTS
- 2006 Newbery Honor Winner
- New York Times Bestseller
- 2006 ALA Notable Children's Book

DISCUSSION QUESTIONS

1. Which Princess Academy girl would you choose as a close friend? Why?
2. Learning quarry-speech helped Miri feel more connected to her community. What helps you feel connected to your community/family/friends?
3. Why did Miri love her mountain so much? Describe something you love about where you live!
4. "The discussion continued, and Miri leaned into her pa, drowsy from watching the fire. *We have linder in our bones*, Doter had said. *We*. Miri clung to the word, wanting to be a part of it but unsure if she was" (141). Why does Miri feel like an outsider in her own community? Do you think Doter meant Miri, too, when she made that comment? Why or why not? How can we help others feel like they belong?
5. Describe a time when Miri was kind, even when she didn't want to be. How did her kind acts help her to be strong when the bandits threatened her friends?
6. Would you choose to stay on Mt. Eskel or move to the lowlands? Why?
7. Why didn't Miri's father tell her the real reason he forbade her from working in the quarry? Was this the right decision? Why or why not?
8. In addition to learning how to read and write, the Mt. Eskel girls also learned about Danlander History, Commerce, Geography, Diplomacy, Conversation, and Poise at the Princess Academy. Which Princess Academy subjects would you like to study? Why?
9. When Miri tells the girls to run away from Olana and her soldiers for spring holiday, she thinks, "Never hesitate if you know it's right" (117). What are some "right" things we should never hesitate to do?
10. Were you surprised by the prince's choice for the princess? Why or why not?

SNACK IDEAS
- **Honeyed nuts**
- **Cabbage soup**
- **Hot tea with honey**
- **Apples, salted and roasted**
- **Oat biscuits with honey**
- **Fruit dusted with sugar**

ACTIVITY IDEAS
- **Poise Lessons**: Practice walking straight with books balanced on your head, learn a deep curtsy and a shallow curtsy, and practice the art of conversation.
- **Ribbon Dance**: Give each girl a long red ribbon and watch a video online to learn a traditional Scandinavian ribbon dance like the girls performed at the Harvest Festival.
- **Diplomacy:** Learn the rules of diplomacy: State the problem. Admit your own error. State the error of the other party. Propose specific compromises. Invite mutual acceptance. Illustrate the negative outcome of refusal and positive of acceptance. Assert a deadline of acceptance. (153-156) Give the girls an example of a conflict between siblings or friends and let them practice negotiating.
- **Dress Up:** Wear fancy princess dresses and hold a pretend ball!
- **Soap Carving:** Give each girl a bar of soap and a plastic knife. Pretend the soap is linder and practice carving the "stone." Try to make a hawk!

FUN FACTS
- Shannon Hale wrote over twelve drafts of this book!
- The food in the book is inspired by medieval Danish cookbooks.
- There are two sequels to the book, *Palace of Stone* and *The Forgotten Sisters*.

IF YOU LIKED THIS BOOK, YOU'LL LOVE...
- *Keeper of the Lost Cities* by Shannon Messenger
- *The True Confessions of Charlotte Doyle* by Avi

PICTURE BOOK SUGGESTIONS
- *A Stone is a Story* by Leslie Barnard Booth
- *The Princess and the Petri Dish* by Sue Fliess

Part 2: The Guide

Princess Academy
Planning Guide

Meeting Date & Time: _____

Host: _____

Rating: ☆☆☆☆☆

Thoughts about the Book:

_____

_____

_____

Snacks:

_____

_____

_____

Activities:

_____

_____

_____

Supplies Needed:

_____

_____

_____

Notes:

_____

_____

_____

How Did It Go?

_____

_____

_____

Future Planning

Next Book: _____

Next Meeting Time: _____

Next Host: _____

Where the Mountain Meets the Moon

by Grace Lin

Stuck in a poor village at the base of Fruitless Mountain, Minli listens to Ma's complaints and Ba's stories. Desperate to heal Ma's sadness, Minli sets off on a journey inspired by Ba's stories—to meet the Old Man of the Moon and ask for a change of fortune. Along the way, she learns many more stories as she comes face-to-face with a dragon, a tiger, and ultimately, herself.

Lin, Grace. *Where the Mountain Meets the Moon*. New York: Little, Brown and Company, 2009.

STATS
- Publisher: Little, Brown and Company
- Originally Published: 2009
- Genre: Fantasy
- Subgenre: Chinese Folklore
- Themes: Gratitude, Family
- Page Count: 278
- Best for Ages: 9+

AWARDS & LISTS
- Newbery Honor
- Mythopoeic Fantasy Award for Children's Literature

DISCUSSION QUESTIONS

1. Which characters end up miserable at the end? Which characters end up happy? What was the difference?
2. Minli and her father could hear the goldfish before Ma could hear them. Why do you think Ma could finally hear the fish in the end?
3. "Fortune was not a house full of gold and jade, but something much more. Something she already had and did not need to change" (259). What was Minli's fortune? What is *your* fortune?
4. How did the twins trick the tiger? How did Minli trick the monkeys? In what ways do greed and selfishness trap us?
5. There were so many different tales in this book! Which were your favorite stories? Why?
6. Do you think Dragon knew the weight he was giving to Minli was actually his pearl? If not, do you think he would have given it to Minli if he'd known? If so, why did he give it away?
7. Stories can be of great value to us, even though they cost nothing. In what ways are stories valuable to you? How do they connect us to each other?
8. The word that brought the secret to happiness was Thankfulness. Why do you think thankfulness is the secret to happiness? Do you agree? Why or why not?
9. All the buffalo boy has is "a dirt floor, a pile of grass for a bed, a muddy buffalo, and a secretive friend. Yet he turned away her copper coin and laughed in the sun. Minli couldn't quite understand it and, somehow, felt ashamed" (159). Why do you think Minli felt ashamed? Why do you think the Buffalo Boy could have so little and still be so happy?
10. How did Minli change throughout the story?

SNACK IDEAS
- **Rice bowls**
- **Peaches**
- **Curled cucumbers**
- **Pink shrimp dumplings**
- **Tea stained eggs**
- **Fluffy steamed buns**

ACTIVITY IDEAS
- **Learn Chinese:** Use a language learning app or the internet to learn common Chinese phrases.
- **Dragon Art:** Dragon was created from a piece of art! Draw, paint, mold out of clay, or paper-mache your own dragon!
- **Red Thread Connections:** Draw or color the members of your family, including extended family. Feel free to use actual photographs! Cut out each person and connect them with a red string.
- **Make a Compass:** Using materials such as a bowl, cork, needle, and magnet, make a homemade compass, like Minli used on her journey.
- **Make a Kite:** Craft kites out of paper, chopsticks, and string. Go outside and try to fly them!

FUN FACTS
- A companion novel, *Starry River of the Sky*, was published in 2014, and a sequel, *When the Sea Turns to Silver*, was published in 2016.
- Grace Lin started writing this book at the request of her ill husband and finished it after he passed away.
- Grace Lin created the artwork in the book. Her main character was inspired by a painting.
- As a child, Grace Lin had a goldfish named Sushi.

IF YOU LIKED THIS BOOK, YOU'LL LOVE...
- *Princess Academy* by Shannon Hale
- *Keeper of the Lost Cities* by Shannon Messenger

PICTURE BOOK SUGGESTIONS
- *A Big Mooncake for Little Star* by Grace Lin
- *Ocean Meets Sky* by The Fan Brothers

Where the Mountain Meets the Moon
Planning Guide

Meeting Date & Time: _____

Host: _____

Rating: ☆☆☆☆☆

Thoughts about the Book:

_____

_____

_____

Snacks:

_____

_____

_____

Activities:

_____

_____

_____

Supplies Needed:

_____

_____

_____

Notes:

_____

_____

_____

How Did It Go?

_____

_____

_____

Future Planning

Next Book: _____

Next Meeting Time: _____

Next Host: _____

Keeper of the Lost Cities
by Shannon Messenger

Sophie knows she's not like everyone else. From her child-prodigy grades to her frustratingly loud mind-reading capabilities, she's always been an outsider. But it's not until she meets Fitz, an elf from the Lost Cities, that she learns just how different she actually is. Not only is Sophie an elf, but she has capabilities even the ancient elves of the Council have never seen. That's scary for someone like Sophie, who just wants to fit in at her new school, the elite Foxfire Academy. Still, the more she learns about the world of elves, the more Sophie realizes that in order to save both human and elvenkind, she'll need to stand out more than ever before.

Messenger, Shannon. *Keeper of the Lost Cities*. New York: Simon & Schuster, 2012.

STATS
- Publisher: Simon & Schuster
- Originally Published: 2012
- Genre: Fantasy
- Subgenre: Adventure
- Themes: Coming of Age, Courage, Friendship, Found Family
- Page Count: 488
- Best for Ages: 9+

AWARDS & LISTS
- New York Times Bestseller
- USA Today Bestseller
- California Young Reader Medal

Mother-Daughter Book Club Guide

DISCUSSION QUESTIONS

1. Do you have a stuffy like Ella? Tell us about it!
2. When faced with the choice of either faking her own death or having her family forget her, Sophie chose the latter to save her family the pain of losing her. Would you have made the same choice as Sophie? Why or why not?
3. What do you think you would *like* about hearing people's thoughts? What *wouldn't* you like about it?
4. Sophie and Fitz can hear thoughts, Dax has mechanical gifts, and Grady and Edaline are gifted with handling creatures. Which special elf power would *you* choose?
5. Time to 'fess up: Team Dax, Fitz, or Keefe? Why?
6. Do you think Sophie will ever get to talk to her parents again? Do you think they'll get a chance to remember her? Why or why not?
7. All Sophie wants is to fit in, but she keeps getting into big trouble. How would you feel if you were in Sophie's situation?
8. When Sophie finds out that Biana was forced to be her friend, she runs to a cave and throws rocks at the wall to vent her frustration. "The clatter as [the rock] shattered into smaller bits was oddly soothing" (416). How do you soothe your emotions when they feel like they are too big to handle?
9. Was Dax a good friend? What about Keefe, Fitz, or Biana? Why or why not?
10. When Tiergan asked Sophie if she missed her human life, "she thought about the headaches, the fear of discovery, how out of place she always felt, and opened her mouth to say, 'No.' But, 'Sometimes I miss my family,' slipped out instead" (324). If you had to start a new life like Sophie, what would you miss most about your life now? What wouldn't you miss?

SNACK IDEAS
- **E.L. Fudge cookies**
- **Lushberry juice:** an elvin drink served in a bright green bottle that tastes sweet and delicious
- **Prattle:** Sweet and chewy caramel peanut butter candy
- Recipes on Shannon Messenger's website:
    - **Mallowmelt**
    - **Mallowmelt Cupcakes**
    - **Fitz's Favorite Chocolate-mint Ripplefluffs**
    - **Sophie's Special Butter-toffee Ripplefluffs**

ACTIVITY IDEAS
- **Prattle Pins:** Create your own pins of real animals or the animals from the book. Collect or trade them, just like the kids at Foxfire Academy!
- **Pathfinders:** Make your own pathfinders by gluing crystals to the end of wooden dowels and decorating them.
- **Ultimate Splotching Championship:** Toss water balloons back and forth until you have a winner! Use colored water or colored powder to make it more like the book.
- **Memory Logs:** Decorate a notebook, then write or draw specific life memories.
- **Find the Crystal:** Sophie had to follow clues in Paris to figure out how to get home. Play a game where the girls must figure out clues to find a hidden "crystal" that will take them home.

FUN FACTS
- There are nine books in the series, with a 10th planned.
- *Keeper of the Lost Cities* was inspired by the X-Men series and Legolas from *The Lord of the Rings*.
- Ella the elephant was based on Shannon Messenger's stuffed animal elephant that she still takes with her everywhere.

IF YOU LIKED THIS BOOK, YOU'LL LOVE…
- *Princess Academy* by Shannon Hale
- *The True Confessions of Charlotte Doyle* by Avi

PICTURE BOOK SUGGESTIONS
- *Through the Fairy Door* by Gabby Dawnay
- *Children of the Forest* by Matthew Myers

Keeper of the Lost Cities

Planning Guide

Meeting Date & Time: _____

Host: _____

Rating: ☆☆☆☆☆

Thoughts about the Book:

_____

_____

_____

Snacks:

_____

_____

_____

Activities:

_____

_____

_____

Supplies Needed:

_____

_____

_____

Notes:

_____

_____

_____

How Did It Go?

_____

_____

_____

Future Planning

Next Book: _____

Next Meeting Time: _____

Next Host: _____

Anne of Green Gables
by L. M. Montgomery

When orphan Anne Shirley first arrives at the Cuthberts' home at Green Gables, she's devastated to hear that siblings Marilla and Matthew Cuthbert had actually requested a boy. Thanks to her indomitable spirit and irresistible imagination, she convinces the reclusive pair to keep her and finally finds a place to call home. But despite Anne's attempts to do good and be good, she ends up in all kinds of scrapes and delightful mishaps, including dying her hair, getting stuck in a sinking rowboat, and falling off a chicken house! Throughout her misadventures, Anne must learn to navigate friendship, family, and what it means to belong.

Montgomery, L. M. *Anne of Green Gables*. New York: Bantam Books, 1908.

STATS
- Publisher: Bantam Books
- Originally Published: 1908
- Genre: Classic
- Subgenre: Family
- Themes: Imagination, Friendship
- Page Count: 276
- Best for Ages: 9+

AWARDS & LISTS
- Has sold more than 50 million copies

DISCUSSION QUESTIONS

1. What does it mean to have a "bosom friend"? Do you have one?
2. How does Anne change as she grows older?
3. Anne gets herself into loads of trouble, like falling off the Barrys' roof, dying her hair green, and getting stuck in a sinking boat! Which was your favorite "Anne Mistake"? Why?
4. How did Matthew and Marilla show Anne that they loved her? How do your friends and family show you they love you? How do you show others you love them?
5. Should Anne have forgiven Gilbert Blythe for calling her Carrots? If she had, would she have done as well as she did in school?
6. Anne loved making up beautiful names for places. Think of a few places in your town. What new names might Anne give them?
7. Despite her difficulties, Anne declares, "But really, Marilla, one can't stay sad very long in such an interesting world, can one?" (137). What do you think Anne means by this? How do you get through sad times in your life?
8. What were Anne's best and worst personality traits? Which characteristics do you like about yourself, and which things are you working to improve?
9. Did Matthew's death surprise you? Do you think Anne made the right decision when she chose to give up college to stay with Marilla?
10. Anne says, "Looking forward to things is half the pleasure of them.... You mayn't get the things themselves; but nothing can prevent you from having the fun of looking forward to them" (94). Rachel Lynde disagrees with Anne's thoughts, insisting that it's better to expect nothing so that you won't be disappointed. Do you side with Anne or Miss Rachel on this topic? Why?

SNACK IDEAS
- **Bread, butter, and crabapple preserves**
- **Tea**
- **Cookies and snaps**
- **Raspberry cordial**
- **Pound cake or layer cake**
- **Cherry pie**

ACTIVITY IDEAS
- **Chalk Slates:** Make your own chalk slates, using old picture frames or frames from the dollar store. Then paint the glass with chalkboard paint!
- **Tea Party:** Dress in fancy clothes, set out fancy food, and enjoy a tea party, just like Anne and her friends!
- **Coded Messages:** Help the girls come up with coded messages, like Anne and Diana did with their candles. Give out flashlights. Then go somewhere dark so the girls can send their messages to each other!
- **Dare Game:** Take turns daring each other to do silly or funny things. Consider making a list of dares that the girls can choose out of a hat. (No dangerous dares allowed!)
- **Recitations:** Memorize short poems and recite them for the group!

FUN FACTS
- Lucy Maud Montgomery sent her *Anne of Green Gables* manuscript to many publishers in 1905 and was rejected by all of them. She put the story away, but pulled it back out in 1907 and sent it off again. A publishing company bought it, and it sold 19,000 copies in the first five months, making it an immediate success.
- L. M. Montgomery wrote 20 novels, two poetry collections, and over 500 short stories.
- *Anne of Green Gables* was inspired by Montgomery's own childhood and young adult experiences.

IF YOU LIKED THIS BOOK, YOU'LL LOVE...
- *The True Confessions of Charlotte Doyle* by Avi
- *Inside Out and Back Again* by Thanhhà Lại

PICTURE BOOK SUGGESTIONS
- *Owl Moon* by Jane Yolen
- *If I Couldn't Be Anne* by Kallie George

Anne of Green Gables
Planning Guide

Meeting Date & Time: _____

Host: _____

Rating: ☆☆☆☆☆

Thoughts about the Book:

_____

_____

_____

Snacks:

_____

_____

_____

Activities:

_____

_____

_____

Supplies Needed:

_____

_____

_____

Notes:

_____

_____

_____

How Did It Go?

_____

_____

_____

Future Planning

Next Book: _____

Next Meeting Time: _____

Next Host: _____

Bridge to Terabithia
by Katherine Patterson

Jess Aarons is determined to be the fastest runner in the fifth grade—until a strange new neighbor girl, Leslie Burke, beats him in a surprise upset. An unexpected friendship develops, and together, Leslie and Jess create a magical world in the woods named Terabithia. In Terabithia, Leslie introduces Jess to a life filled with imagination and possibilities. Then tragedy strikes, and Jess must learn how to navigate his newfound awareness while enduring the profound loss of his best friend.

Paterson, Katherine. *Bridge to Terabithia*. New York: HarperCollins, 1977.

STATS
- Publisher: HarperCollins
- Originally Published: 1977
- Genre: Classic
- Subgenre: Realistic Fiction
- Themes: Grief, Friendship
- Page Count: 208
- Best for Ages: 9+

AWARDS & LISTS
- 1978 Newbery Medal

DISCUSSION QUESTIONS

1. Why is Terabithia so important to Jess and Leslie?
2. How does Leslie's friendship help Jess? How does Jess's friendship help Leslie?
3. Leslie's parents claim they moved to the country for Leslie's sake, but Jess disagrees. What do you think?
4. How does meeting Leslie affect Jess's relationship with his father and younger sister May Belle? Think of your relationships—have you ever improved a relationship with someone you loved? What changed?
5. Jess and Leslie get revenge on Janice Avery by writing a fake love letter from her crush, Willard. Does Janice Avery deserve the punishment Leslie and Jess give her? Why or why not?
6. Think of something hard you've experienced that made you stronger. Tell us about it!
7. At the end of the novel, Jess tells his little sister, "Everybody gets scared sometimes, May Belle. You don't have to be ashamed" (123). What does Jess mean by this? What do you get scared about? When you feel scared, how do you handle it?
8. Jess knows that a puppy will be the perfect gift for Leslie, just like Leslie knows Jess will love a real paint set. Describe a gift that meant a lot to you—either that you received or that you gave. What made it so special?
9. "Before Leslie came, he had been a nothing.... It was Leslie who had taken him from the cow pasture into Terabithia and turned him into a king" (126). What does this mean? What can we learn from Jess's experience?
10. Why is racing so important to Jess at the beginning of the book? How does his attitude change after meeting—and then losing—Leslie?

SNACK IDEAS
- **Twinkies**
- **Dried fruit**
- **Crackers**
- **Pancakes**

ACTIVITY IDEAS
- **Silly Animal Drawings:** Draw silly animals like Jess does at the beginning of the book.
- **Movie Time:** Get comfy and watch the movie! (Our favorite version came out in 2007.)
- **Relay Races:** Plan and participate in various relay races, such as a running race, a three-legged race, a galloping race, etc.
- **Create Your Own Terabithia:** In your house or backyard, encourage the girls to create their own magical kingdom. Have them walk across a plank or swing on a rope to get to their special place. If you can't go outside, build a fort under a table or make a diorama of Terabithia!
- **Wreath-making:** Make wreaths to honor a loved one who has passed on, or make them as a gift for someone else who has lost a loved one, like Jess did for Leslie.

FUN FACTS
- The story of this book was inspired by Katherine Paterson's son's friend, who died after being struck by lightning.
- Katherine Paterson also won the Newbery for *Jacob Have I Loved* in 1981. *The Great Gilly Hopkins* received a Newbery Honor and won the National Book Award in 1979.
- Katherine Paterson has written over forty books!
- Katherine Paterson wanted to be either a movie star or a missionary when she was a child.

IF YOU LIKED THIS BOOK, YOU'LL LOVE...
- *Out of My Mind* by Sharon M. Draper
- *The True Confessions of Charlotte Doyle* by Avi

PICTURE BOOK SUGGESTIONS
- *Wherever You Are, My Love Will Find You* by Nancy Tillman
- *The Invisible String* by Patrice Karst

Bridge to Terabithia
Planning Guide

Meeting Date & Time: _____

Host: _____

Rating: ☆☆☆☆☆

Thoughts about the Book:

_____

_____

_____

Snacks:

_____

_____

_____

Activities:

_____

_____

_____

Supplies Needed:

_____

_____

_____

Notes:

_____

_____

_____

How Did It Go?

_____

_____

_____

Future Planning

Next Book:_____

Next Meeting Time:_____

Next Host:_____

Part 2: The Guide

I Am Malala:
How One Girl Stood Up for Education and Changed the World, Young Readers Edition
by Malala Yousafzai with Patricia McCormick

Fifteen-year-old Malala Yousafzai's life changed forever when she was shot by Taliban soldiers on her way home from school. Malala tells the story of how she became an outspoken supporter of girl's education in Pakistan—even though it made her a target for the Taliban. She introduces readers to her parents, pesky brothers, best friends, and mentors, as well as the wild mountains and noisy streets of her beloved Pakistan. No matter how far Malala's voice travels or how many awards she receives, she reminds us that she will always be Malala.

Yousafzai, Malala and Patricia McCormick. *I Am Malala: How One Girl Stood Up for Education and Changed the World*. New York: Little, Brown and Company, 2014.

STATS
- Publisher: Little, Brown and Company
- Originally Published: 2014
- Genre: Nonfiction
- Subgenre: Memoir
- Themes: Social Justice, Family
- Page Count: 256
- Best for Ages: 10+

AWARDS & LISTS
- The Amelia Bloomer Booklist
- International Literacy Association Teachers' Choice
- CBC Children's Choice Book Award Finalist

DISCUSSION QUESTIONS

1. Malala is a world leader, but she's also an everyday-girl who argues with her brothers and giggles with her friends. In what ways are you like Malala?
2. How does the Taliban believe females should be treated? Why do you think Malala's dad was willing to risk his life to educate girls in Pakistan?
3. "My mother loved schoolwork even more than I did, if that was possible. My father said it was because she had been deprived of learning for so long" (120). Why do you think education meant so much to Malala's mother?
4. After the earthquake, Malala explains, "The whole country was in shock....We were vulnerable. Which made it that much easier for someone with bad intentions to use a nation's fear against them" (31). Why are people more likely to make unwise decisions if they are scared?
5. How would you feel if you lived under Taliban rule?
6. What does Malala love about Pakistan? What do you love about the place where you live?
7. "It's odd to be so well-known but to be lonely at the same time" (177). Why do you think Malala feels lonely sometimes?
8. Why did Malala's family leave Pakistan and move to England? If it were safe, do you think they would choose to return home to Pakistan? Why or why not?
9. "I think of the world as a family. When one of us is suffering, we must all pitch in and help" (188). Are there problems in your community or school that need to be solved? What can you do to help?
10. When Malala attends school in England, she realizes, "What I'm finding is that we have much more in common than we have different, and every day, we learn something new from one another" (181). What have you learned from people who are different from you?

SNACK IDEAS
- **Tea**
- **Chapati bread**
- **Fried eggs**
- **Toffee**
- **Cake**

ACTIVITY IDEAS
- **Outdoor Games:** Play the games Malala played with her brothers—cricket, a chasing game (like tag), chindakh (hopscotch), or parpartuni (hide & seek).
- **I Am _____:** Draw self portraits and write "I am (your name)" underneath it. Ask the girls to think about what it means to be themselves. Encourage them to write or draw things they like about themselves.
- **Speak Up:** Give the girls an opportunity to prepare a one-minute speech about something they care about. Let them take turns giving their speeches to the rest of the group, who should act as if they were members of the United Nations.
- **Fundraiser:** Plan a fundraiser and donate the money earned to the Malala Fund.
- **Watch Malala's Speech:** Watch a recording of Malala's speech at the United Nations. Discuss what you learned from her speech.

FUN FACTS
- In October 2014, Malala was awarded the Nobel Peace Prize. At 17 years old, she was the youngest person to ever receive it!
- Malala launched the Malala Fund, which funds education projects to empower girls.
- Patricia McCormick is an award-winning author who has published several other books about young people who must defy impossible odds.

IF YOU LIKED THIS BOOK, YOU'LL LOVE...
- *Out of My Mind* by Sharon M. Draper
- *Inside Out and Back Again* by Thanhhà Lại

PICTURE BOOK SUGGESTIONS
- *Malala's Magic Pencil* by Malala Yousafzai
- *Speak Up* by Miranda Paul

I Am Malala
Planning Guide

Meeting Date & Time: _____

Host: _____

Rating: ☆☆☆☆☆

Thoughts about the Book:

_____

_____

_____

Snacks:

_____

_____

_____

Activities:

_____

_____

_____

Supplies Needed:

_____

_____

_____

Notes:

_____

_____

_____

How Did It Go?

_____

_____

_____

Future Planning

Next Book: _____

Next Meeting Time: _____

Next Host: _____

Yummy: A History of Desserts
by Victoria Grace Elliott

Join Peri, Fada, and Fee, a trio of food sprites, on a trip around the world and through time—all in the name of desserts! From the beginnings of pie to the origins of cake, gummies, and even ice cream, the sprites share historical milestones, tell food legends, and even teach the science behind some of our favorite sweet treats.

Elliott, Victoria Grace. *Yummy: A History of Desserts.* New York, Random House, 2021.

STATS
- Publisher: Random House Graphic
- Originally Published: 2021
- Genre: Nonfiction
- Subgenre: Graphic Novel
- Themes: General Knowledge, Food
- Page Count: 240
- Best for Ages: 9+

AWARDS & LISTS
- 2022 Excellence in Graphic Literature Award

DISCUSSION QUESTIONS

1. What is your favorite kind of dessert? Would you like to try a treat from another country?
2. Early cakes took forever to make—just beating the eggs lasted an hour! What kind of food would you be willing to spend hours preparing?
3. In what ways did advances in science affect cake-baking history? How does science affect baking today?
4. "Hot, cool, after dinner, or as an afternoon snack, cookies are the perfect small treat!" says Peri (211). Do you agree? What is your favorite small treat? When do you eat them?
5. No one really knows where the donut hole came from. Can your book club group come up with your own legend?
6. Some of the first pies were more like containers made of hard crust and filled with all sorts of ingredients, including live creatures! What would you put in your ancient pie?
7. Cream, fruit, or meat pie? Which do you think is the best—and why?
8. "Desserts aren't always what they seem.... And neither is history!" say Fada and Fee (226). What is one thing that surprised you when learning about dessert history?
9. "History is so big, and I'm so small!" (226). Peri wishes she could include even more food history—there's so much to choose from! Which food history topics would you like to learn more about? Why?
10. The English word "cookie" likely comes from the Dutch word "koekji." What are some other food names that might have come from other countries?

SNACK IDEAS

Many of these recipes can be found in the book! See page numbers in the descriptions.

- **Ice Cream:** ice cream sundaes, waffle cones, bastani sonnati, bingsu, fried ice cream, coconut milk ice cream, gelato, ice cream cake, halo-halo, kulfi, mochi
  - ◇ Easy Ice Cream Recipe (44)
- **Cake:** mooncake, gugelhupf, pound cake, sponge cake, castella cake, pandan cake, chocolate torte, cake mix, red velvet cake, carrot cake, sfouf, ghevar, bibingka
  - ◇ Funfetti Cake Recipe (93)
- **Brownies**
- **Donuts:** jalebi, mardi gras donuts, sufganiyot, churros, beignets, calzones rotos, picarones, olie koeken, donut holes
- **Pie:** fruit pie (apple, blueberry, cherry), vegetable pie (pumpkin, sweet potato), egg tart, custard pie (pecan, key lime), empanada
  - ◇ Blueberry Pie Recipe (165)
- **Gummies:** gumdrops, gummy bears
- **Cookies:** biscotti, nankhatai, madeleines, shortbread, chocolate chip
  - ◇ Snickerdoodles Recipe (209)
- **Macarons**

ACTIVITY IDEAS
Many of these activities can be found in the book! See page numbers in the descriptions.

- **Salt & Ice Experiment:** Science Lab (23)
- **Leavening: Baking Powder or Baking Soda:** Science Lab (pg. 64)
- **Pastry Dough & Butter Pockets:** Science Lab (133)
- **Decorate Cupcakes**
- **Dessert Art:** Mold and paint your favorite desserts out of air dry clay!
- **TV Cooking Show:** Work in teams to create a TV cooking show video as you prepare a dessert from the book!

FUN FACTS
- A companion novel, *Tasty: A History of Yummy Experiments,* was published in 2023.
- Victoria Grace Elliott used sprites to narrate the story because she wanted the desserts to seem big. The little sprites were the perfect size to do that.
- Elliott writes, draws, colors, and letters everything on her own. (Sometimes multiple people create these different parts of a graphic novel!)
- Elliott's favorite dessert is crème brûlée or chocolate mousse.

IF YOU LIKED THIS BOOK, YOU'LL LOVE...
- *Smile* by Raina Telgemeier
- *Anne of Green Gables* by L. M. Montgomery

PICTURE BOOK SUGGESTIONS
- *Edible Crafts Kids' Cookbook* by Charity Mathews
- *The Complete Baking Book for Young Chefs* by America Test Kitchen Kids

Yummy: A History of Desserts
Planning Guide

Meeting Date & Time: _____

Host: _____

Rating: ☆☆☆☆☆

Thoughts about the Book:

_____

_____

_____

Snacks:

_____

_____

_____

Activities:

_____

_____

_____

Supplies Needed:

_____

_____

_____

Notes:

_____

_____

_____

How Did It Go?

_____

_____

_____

Future Planning

Next Book: _____

Next Meeting Time: _____

Next Host: _____

Appendix

Appendix

INDEX

Books By Genre
- Adventure
    - *The True Confessions of Charlotte Doyle* 13
    - *Princess Academy* 43
    - *Where the Mountain Meets the Moon* 49
    - *Keeper of the Lost Cities* 55
- Classic
    - *Anne of Green Gables* 61
    - *Bridge to Terabithia* 67
- Fantasy
    - *Princess Academy* 43
    - *Where the Mountain Meets the Moon* 49
    - *Keeper of the Lost Cities* 55
- Graphic Novel
    - *Smile* 37
    - *Yummy: A History of Desserts* 79
- Historical Fiction
    - *The True Confessions of Charlotte Doyle* 13
    - *Inside Out and Back Again* 19
- Mystery
    - *The True Confessions of Charlotte Doyle* 13
    - *Three Times Lucky* 31
- Nonfiction/Memoir
    - *Smile* 37
    - *I Am Malala* 73
    - *Yummy: A History of Desserts* 79
- Novel in Verse
    - *Inside Out and Back Again* 19
- Realistic Fiction
    - *Out of My Mind* 25
    - *Three Times Lucky* 31
    - *Anne of Green Gables* 61
    - *Bridge to Terabithia* 67

Books By Topic

- Believing in Yourself
    - *The True Confessions of Charlotte Doyle* 13
    - *Out of My Mind* 25
    - *Princess Academy* 43
    - *Keeper of the Lost Cities* 55
    - *Bridge to Terabithia* 67
    - *I Am Malala* 73
- Bullying
    - *Inside Out and Back Again* 19
    - *Out of My Mind* 25
    - *Princess Academy* 43
    - *Smile* 37
    - *Bridge to Terabithia* 67
- Chinese Folklore
    - *Where the Mountain Meets the Moon* 49
- Class
    - *The True Confessions of Charlotte Doyle* 13
    - *Princess Academy* 43
    - *Where the Mountain Meets the Moon* 49
    - *Keeper of the Lost Cities* 55
    - *Yummy: A History of Desserts* 79
- Coming-of-Age
    - *The True Confessions of Charlotte Doyle* 13
    - *Smile* 37
    - *Princess Academy* 43
    - *Where the Mountain Meets the Moon* 49
    - *Keeper of the Lost Cities* 55
    - *Anne of Green Gables* 61
    - *Bridge to Terabithia* 67
    - *I Am Malala* 73
- Community
    - *Three Times Lucky* 31
    - *Princess Academy* 43
    - *Anne of Green Gables* 61

- Courage
  - *The True Confessions of Charlotte Doyle* 13
  - *Inside Out and Back Again* 19
  - *Out of My Mind* 25
  - *Three Times Lucky* 31
  - *Princess Academy* 43
  - *Where the Mountain Meets the Moon* 49
  - *Keeper of the Lost Cities* 55
  - *I Am Malala* 73
- Culture
  - *Inside Out and Back Again* 19
  - *Where the Mountain Meets the Moon* 49
  - *I Am Malala* 73
- Disabilities
  - *Out of My Mind* 25
- Diversity
  - *Inside Out and Back Again* 19
  - *Out of My Mind* 25
  - *I Am Malala* 73
  - *Yummy: A History of Desserts* 79
- Education
  - *Inside Out and Back Again* 19
  - *Princess Academy* 43
  - *Anne of Green Gables* 61
  - *I Am Malala* 73
- Family
  - *Inside Out and Back Again* 19
  - *Three Times Lucky* 31
  - *Where the Mountain Meets the Moon* 49
  - *Anne of Green Gables* 61
  - *I Am Malala* 73
- Found Family
  - *Three Times Lucky* 31
  - *Keeper of the Lost Cities* 55
  - *Anne of Green Gables* 61

- Friendship
  - *Inside Out and Back Again* 19
  - *Out of My Mind* 25
  - *Three Times Lucky* 31
  - *Smile* 37
  - *Princess Academy* 43
  - *Keeper of the Lost Cities* 55
  - *Anne of Green Gables* 61
  - *Bridge to Terabithia* 67
- Gratitude
  - *Inside Out and Back Again* 19
  - *Where the Mountain Meets the Moon* 49
- Grief
  - *Bridge to Terabithia* 67
- Imagination
  - *Anne of Green Gables* 61
  - *Bridge to Terabithia* 67
- Immigrant Story
  - *Inside Out and Back Again* 19
  - *I Am Malala* 73
- Inclusion
  - *Inside Out and Back Again* 19
  - *Out of My Mind* 25
  - *Smile* 37
  - *Princess Academy* 43
  - *I Am Malala* 73
- Kindness
  - *Inside Out and Back Again* 19
  - *Out of My Mind* 25
  - *Smile* 37
  - *Princess Academy* 43
  - *Where the Mountain Meets the Moon* 49

ABOUT THE AUTHORS

Meghan Voss, M.Ed.

Meghan Voss loves reading, teaching, and helping kids write! She earned a B.A. in English from Brigham Young University and a Masters in Secondary Education from the University of Maryland. A former high school English teacher, Meghan has published magazine articles and blog posts, edited everything from dissertations to picture books, and currently works as an education manager with a local non-profit organization. When Meghan isn't geeking out over books and literature, you can find her lifting weights, hiking, and picking fresh huckleberries for homemade pie. Meghan lives in northwest Montana with her husband, three children, and the occasional bear that strolls through her backyard.

Stefanie Hohl, M.Ed., MFA

Stefanie Hohl loves books, book clubs, and writing books for kids! She is the author of *The Remember Tree*, *Where is the Star*, and the ABC See, Hear, Do series, a learn-to-read program that uses movement to teach early reading skills. She holds a Masters in Education in Curriculum and Instruction from Penn State, as well as a Masters of Fine Arts in Writing for Children and Young Adults from Vermont College of Fine Arts. When Stefanie isn't planning book clubs, she loves to run, snowboard, and bake peanut butter bars. Stefanie lives in Pittsburgh with her husband, five children, two very silly dogs, and two cuddly cats.

www.ingramcontent.com/pod-product-compliance
Lightning Source LLC
Chambersburg PA
CBHW061739070526
44585CB00024B/2740